CW00959195

'rocrast E

by Tony Wood

Tony Wood rides a skateboard, drives a train and helped build a thousand-plus online community of skateboarders forging hundreds of new friendships, collaborations, and opportunities.
In short, he helped create a Family of UK Skateboarders.

He is owned and managed by Mertle Wood.

The dark and unknown forces of the universe converged on Tony to coerce him to forge his skate-related penmanship into this anthology.

:: artwork ::
Arron Campbell, Jason
'Hillbilly' Cheverall, Dan Bryant

Procrastiskate

by Tony Wood

First published in the UK in 2020 by Stour Valley Publishing

The images in this book have been produced by Jason 'Hillbilly' Cheverall, Arron Campbell, and Dan Bryant

Cover Image: © Jason 'Hillbilly' Cheverall

A CIP Catalogue Record of this book is available from the British Library

ISBN: 978-1-913450-01-4 (PB)

Printed & Bound by Mixam UK Ltd, Watford, UK

Stour Valley Publishing
3 Tiberius Close
Haverhill
CB9 0NP
www.stourvalleypublishing.co.uk

SVP
STOUR VALLEY
PUBLISHING

This book is for Sonya who is more than I could ever deserve.

It is for Mum and Dad who have always supported my writing, regardless of its quality

It is for Hillbilly, Arron, Dan and Carl without whom it simply wouldn't exist

It is for FoUKS, the Teabeggers, and for skateboarding.

oreword

by Carl Mynott

When I asked Tony who it was that he wanted to write the foreword for Procrastiskate I got super excited that I would be editing and placing the words from someone truly awesome. Given that Tony is connected with some of the foremost pro-skaters of the nineties I was squeaking with anticipation of someone like Sean Goff, Don Brider, or maybe Frankie Hill... Yep, FRANKIE HILL!!!
On the flip he might go with one of the more contemporary rippers in his friends list; Jordan Thackeray, Jesse Thomas, Joe Hinson... but no. No!

The wombat chose me!

To my mind, it was an odd choice, yet I love him for it. You see, I think I can take a little credit for nagging him enough to do something permanent, and something special with his writing. And it was something I could help him make a reality. So... not only am I over the moon to have Tony on the books as one of Stour Valley Publishing's first titles, but I am also super-stoked to be writing this foreword.

Skateboarding for me was everything when I was a kid, and it took me well into my teens, too. But, with the pressures of the expectation of others, I stopped practising as I grew older and 'wiser'. There were more adulty things I should be doing - like working. And dadding. And going to dinner with friends. You can't keep skating when you are supposed to be 'grown-up'. But. you will see, this book proves that all of this is, roundly, bollocks. You can... no... YOU MUST carry on skating as you get older. Notice the moment that folk begin to expect you to not be skating any more. You know, because it's not the done thing at your age... and... show them this book. Then, give them a few minutes for it to sink in before flicking them a hearty (yet respectful) "Fuck you!". Then hop on your board and nail the three-set at the front of their house.

Contents

Introduction

My name is Tony...

My name is Tony (which I figure you already guessed due to the name 'Tony' being emblazoned on the cover of this anthology) and I have always loved to write.

Poetry and rhymes seem to come very easily to me and generally involve a minimum amount of effort. I write from the heart and never really do second drafts, I kid myself that this is because it's 'art' but it's more truthful to say I'm lazy!

My mum and dad always said I should write a book but I dismissed it as just parents being nice and never felt that I had what it takes. A few years ago I started dumping some of my garbled ramblings on Facebook and, specifically, in skateboarding groups. Quite a few people seemed to like them and suggested I collect them together to do a book. I graciously thanked them and laughed at the absurdity of the idea! Eventually, Carl Mynott nagged me into doing this and now you're reading it (so please, blame him).

I hope you find at least some of the following musings funny, moving or at least passable.

So there's the intro. It's longer than I intended but, according to my publisher, just writing 'I'm a bellend that likes rhymes' wouldn't be sufficient! (See, Mat Lloyd? I did it!).

Illustration: Jason "Hillbilly" Cheverall

A lifelong obsession with almost no progression;
perhaps I need a lesson?

For I feel like such a wally when I try to pop an ollie
but it's wonky, weak and wobbly!

And every rock fakie is nothing but a maybe
that I crash out of daily.

Not sure that I belong, I get it all so wrong but my knee
slides are the bomb!

You'd expect me to be rad if you looked at my knee pads,
but the truth is, I'm just bad!

I've been skating quite a while, I've no ability, grace or style
I mostly end up in a pile!

Yet I've still got so much pride each time I carve frontside
and manage not to die!

Or I look at my collection, my lovely lady selection and I get
a huge...
warm glowing feeling inside.

Fly

We ponder, we reminisce and think of days gone by
Of how our knees never ached after we'd flown so high

It's in our nature to sit and think
And share good times over a drink

But better than that is to live new days
As older men with a fresh new graze

Chatting in the pub about what we just did
And appreciate more than when we were kids!

For now, we know that times rolls past
So, every chance, just have a blast

For in the morning, you might just find
That fate's a bitch and most unkind

Life's too short to wait and see
So, grab your boards and fly so free.

Scream at Monster and curse Red Bull
Swear at the Olympics for being uncool.
Tear down the Palace and hate on Supreme
Destroy Mountain Dew and piss in their stream.
Just don't do it Nike, fuck off. Reebok
Take your corporate bullshit and suck on my cock!

Or...

Who really cares? Who gives a toss?
Do what you want, be your own boss
Get over yourself and your misguided pride
Just appreciate each day when you get a chance to ride
Let councils throw their money at second rate parks
Let the new dawn break as we skate into the dark
Where were you when skating was only for fools?
I ignored all the piss taking when I skated to school
Skateboarders skateboard and they always will
Not here for fashion, we're here for the thrill!

Misguided Pride

Newtrition

Looking back to a time when I lacked ambition
Didn't give a fuck about correct nutrition
When every sunny day was a brand-new mission
For whole weekends we'd just go missing!

Skating to a place from spot to spot
Showing each other what was what
Riding like maniacs trying to fly
Imitating Barbee's no-comply

Session for hours on a single curb
Ollying drains and fat dog turds
Bombing Ilford hill making cars swerve
Security guards got on our nerves!

We never needed big skate parks
We just hit London's landmarks
Blown away by Stu's street plants
Skated all day 'til it got dark

Those halcyon days were the best I had
I miss those times and it makes me sad
Public Domain was so fucking rad
On rainy days that drove us mad

But now I'm back on a board again
I skate with a whole new bunch of friends
I hope this summer never ends
Yeah, I hope this summer never ends!

Illustration: Jason "Hillbilly" Cheverall

Not designed

Oh, ramp why do you mock me?

I just want a frontside rock see?

In profile you look like you're smiling

As on to your ply my fat body is piling!

Ability? I haven't an ounce!

And I just don't fucking bounce!

You pull my legs apart

Like a badly treated tart

And to prove you are a rotter

You fuck me good and proper!

But to this abuse I'll return

Determined to never learn

That I'm not designed for skating

But I find it liberating.

Our relationship is complex

Just you, me and a deck.

You're such a fucking tease!

Letting others ride you with ease.

It's getting on my nerves

That I'll never tame your curves.

They never said no, they just slightly shook their heads and gave a pitying half smile.

They never really believed that the fat man would do it anyway. Who would? The entire idea was so ludicrous to them that it was beneath contempt or any real contemplation at all.

People were always saying that they were going to do something but they very rarely actually carried through with their ill thought out, half planned schemes.

So, they never really considered it necessary to actually say no.

So, I did it.

I fucking did it!

I got back on a skateboard after a ten-year absence.

In my absence everything and nothing had changed. Skateparks had popped up everywhere but were full of brats on obscene little scooters, skateboard decks and wheels had bounced around various sizes like a fat bloke on a bungee jump and giant online shops, energy drinks and mass produced sport shoes had tried to fuck skateboarding up the arse!

But the core was still there.

The love of skating still burned in the eyes of the sweaty guys at skate only nights. They still gave equal cheer to a fat man dropping in

for the first time in a decade as they did to the gifted whizz kid landing

tricks I couldn't even understand.

My elbow broke.
For about an hour I thought about walking away.
That was over a year ago.
Bones fix. They heal up.
To paraphrase a legend

'You don't quit skating because you're broken, you're broken because you quit skating'.

I don't know if I'll roll forever but guys like Goff, Kizz and Big Woody inspire me to do my best.

I can't see myself ever walking away from skating willingly.
I need to roll. It's part of me and I hope/fear it always will be.

Illustration: Arron Campbell

Why do you walk like that, like everything aches?

Because everything does, because I love to skate!

Why do you have toys adorning your walls?

Because they represent my life, they are art and they are cool!

But you're a fully grown man, you're too old to be playing!

Can't you hear yourself; can you hear what you are saying?

You've got a mortgage to pay, what if you break a bone?

What if I stay indoors and slowly die alone?

Or perhaps go to the pub and get pissed out of my head

And cheer bunch of blokes kicking a ball around instead?

I could take up golf or buy a big red car!

Or have a sad affair with that blonde in the bar!

Yeah, I could quit skating if I really fucking tried

I did it once before but a piece of me died!

I won't stop skating just because I'm old

But I'll age rapidly if I do as I am told!

So just to be clear; this is where I stand

On a fucking skateboard, as a free man!

A skater's what I am
And skating's what I do
And if you do not like it
I guess that that's fine too

But if you try and stop me
I'll just push twice as hard
And if you criticise me
I'll ignore your disregard

For I'm not pushing drugs
Or peddling outside schools
I'm not having drunken fights
Or getting in bar brawls

I'm not smashing up a train
In support of my football team
Or pissing in shop doorways
I'm not drunk or obscene

I'm not rebellious or crazy
Or trying to be cool
I'm just a fat old man
Playing on his skateboard

And that's all I've ever needed

To truly be at peace

Just rollin on some wood

For my stress relief

So next time that I pass you

Just skating down the lane

Take but just a moment

Bite your tongue and refrain

From shouting 'do an ollie'

Or the classic 'Tony Hawk!'

Or you may find my deck

Rammed in your face as you squawk!

For there's only so much abuse

There is an upper limit

I'll roll you to the sea

And put you fucking in it!

Enemy Ebb

It ebbs

It flows

It laps at the shore of your consciousness

It rolls

It rumbles

It raps on the door of total bliss

It hurts

It soothes

It takes no prisoners

Mind and matter

Exterminate chatter

You can not be a visitor

It's calm

It's harsh

Drop to oblivion so insane

No pain

No gain

Have to pay to play this game

No outsiders
Just residers
It holds with warm embrace

Cross fields
Wade lakes
To find the perfect place

You glide
You flow
Nothing to prove or show

Your pride
Your glow
Because you alone can know

It's rewards
It's charms
It's sudden treachery

Such pain
Such joy
That most welcome enemy

Illustration: Jason "Hillbilly" Cheve

he Push

The push between the tricks
The freedom of each kick
The journey on the way
That's the essence of our play

It's not the bolts on every landing
Not the falling not the slamming
It's getting up from when you're down
It's that blessed click-clack sound

It's not who's best or who goes higher
It's the joy in every trier
It's standing on wood strapped to wheels
Only skaters know those thrills

It's not shapes or pops or slicks
It's not ollies or kick flips
It's not blunts or nose picks
It's the push between the tricks

It stirred within his chest, gentle at first but soon gnawing its way into his consciousness. Skater had suppressed the dreaded fat form of Driver for half a decade or more but every winter he felt him fighting back. The negativity, the jowly chops, the surly disposition and the air of cynicism would try to bubble to the surface. 'I'm still here' Driver's voice would hiss into his mind 'and you can't hide me forever!'

'I need to skate' whispered the old man dressed like a kid in need of a stern talking to, 'I must get outside'

Driver had given his host's body a reasonable life. He'd taken it on very many missions over years and even introduced it to people that had become friends but when Skater started to fight for supremacy it had changed everything. Host had started to hate Driver, he detested how Driver was all consuming, he wouldn't let Host be anything other than Driver and was a jealous and petty bastard. Skater had saved Host in every way a man could be saved, a bit like Jack Dawson but with much worse hair really.

At first Skater had only emerged as a kind of ironic embrace to times long past but that had morphed, it had grown and flourished until Skater became the dominant driving force within Host. He had given Host new friends, new experiences and even better health, apart from all the scabs and stuff.

In the dry months of summer Skater flourished. It was his time to shine and Driver hid away in the shadows of Host's mind. But winter was different. The cold, wet streets and parks of Host's world were anathema to the desires of Skater and his dominance was threatened. Perhaps tomorrow would be dry? Maybe Boda or Rumbles would be up for a laugh? Skater smiled at the thought of the tiles and frontside carves.

'Oh, grow up' hissed Driver, 'just grow up and accept the darkness'
'Oh, do piss off' laughed Skater, 'this ain't your Host anymore'

Pebble

Pebble was pissed off. Seriously pissed off! He'd spent the last two hours languishing in the gutter after being kicked down the road by a spotty youth.

'There must be more to life than this'
He grumbled.

He felt the rotten leaves against his back and was horribly aware of the tiny bit of dog poo that was stuck to his cheek. Fighting back gravelly tears, he tried to go to his happy place. Those long summers on the beach, relaxing in the sun as the tide lapped all around him. He remembered how he'd dreamed of becoming a Skimmer and he truly believed that it would happen one day. Of course, this was long before The Bitch had plucked him from the sand and dumped him unceremoniously into a bucket of crabs, shells and sea weed!

Pebble was snapped from his revelry by the best sound any tiny stone could dream of within an urban environment. A skateboard was approaching! That meant a skater was coming.

Timing was everything as the 'clack-clackety-clack' of polyurethane on paving slabs drew closer.

'Wait for it... wait for it' he urged himself.

Suddenly, and with a Herculean effort, he launched himself into the path of the fat giant as he bore down upon him.

The roar was deafening as the once mighty wheel stopped turning and Pebble screamed with delight as he was dragged a full three inches along the pavement. The fat giant was catapulted across the floor and his knees exploded into glorious claret as they smashed to the Tarmac.

Suddenly Pebble was a lot happier.

Southbank

In a piss-stained corner where foxes go to die
On broken city slabs you can hear them cry

Where pavement meets wall and both are cracking
A distant sound, a peculiar 'clacking'

Not to be used as designers foresaw
Rules ripped up; boundaries ignored

A handrail that developed odd little warts
Doesn't stop them coming, these skate stalwarts

Buildings and plazas were never so designed
For how they're viewed now by our fucked-up minds

Twisted up hips, broken feet, torn flesh
Pushing ever further for spots that are fresh

Contrarily benign this cancer in our towns
Wants to herd us into parks and to grind us all down

Illustration: Arron Campbell

Now I'm no rebel, I'm not here to disturb
Just leave me be while I play with this curb

There's fag butts and filth, gum littered all around
But it's me you persecute? For my strange 'clacking' sound?

It's me that spikes your rage and it's my joy you can't handle
This middle-aged kid that you're convinced is a vandal

The truth of your anger is there to see
It's not fuelled by hate, it's just jealousy!

You're jealous of my freedom, you're jealous of my smile
You're jealous of the fun that I have for a while.
You're jealous of the fact that I won't be contained
Within parameters you made so others can be blamed!

But I'll never sink to your exhibited lows
I won't raise my voice or laugh at your clothes
I won't join in with your pitiful hate
I'll smile and I'll wink and I'll go for a skate.

Ennui

There was a passion that he left to starve
It wasted away while he drank in bars
Faithful yet forlorn it sheltered in a chamber
Of a mind wracked and torn, to itself it was a stranger

He packed away his childish toys to history unspoken
But they whispered tales of joy in that mind that was
broken.

People came and women went
His heart got hurt but would always mend
Yet the scars itched still
For that certain thrill.

Time ticked by and he settled down
Wouldn't let his ennui make him frown
A job, a wife, a house, the works
His life grew fine with all its perks
A tapestry, a smorgasbord, a layered cake!!!
Contentment and comfort but something fake.

That sealed up chamber scratched away
Whispered memories of the joy of play
He blocked it off and shut it tight
Until that damn did burst one night!

He'd browsed Facebook until he'd stumbled
Across a rabbit hole down which he'd tumbled!

That well was full of mates and packed with fools
Who embraced the joy of their Skateboards

Now it's bars that are kept in his vacant chamber
As that man-child seeks a better danger.
Yeah there's bones to break and skin to lose
But himself to find outside the booze.

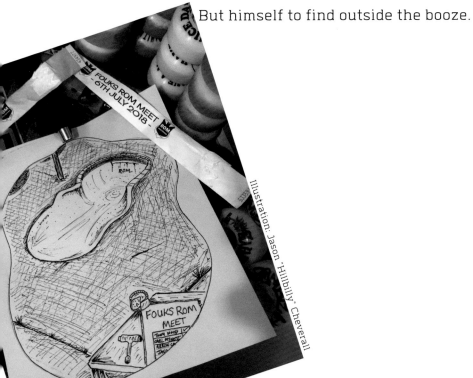

Illustration: Jason 'Hillbilly' Cheverall

Now what

Every day a different bit cracks

These joints are a-popping with mighty cracks

A knees-up with ya mates is all very well

But by Christ Almighty I can really tell

The next day there are bangs and aching bits

But for the love of rolling, it's well worth it.

I sit here now at work and wonder what I've done

To stop my arm from raising

Oh, woe is me

With my painful knee

And sporadic cramps

Brought about by ramps

But I still feel free

Guide-rope

When it's all too much, when your rope's too long
When you're wracked with doubt cos you don't belong

When the only choice left is just to opt out
When the world is deaf to your scream or shout

Know we are here, that we have your back
Turn to your friends to take up the slack

The choice you make will last forever
Don't remove the chance for things to get better!

Don't surrender.
Don't fight alone.
Lean on us
For the journey home.

Take our hands
Accept support
Life is precious
So, don't get caught.

Caught in lies told by your mind
Can make the world appear so unkind

But it truly isn't!

Yeah life can be challenging
And Christ knows it hurts!
But avoid the void
Of no self worth!

Reach out for someone
Reach out for something
For if you don't raise your hand
You may never be seen

Herded

We are herded into parks
Forced to play out in the dark
Our rails have grown lumpen
Beaten back by council truncheons
We traipse to council fields
We're destroyed by shoddy builds
From streets we've been evicted
As social nuisance we're convicted
They keep us all contained
No freedom left to play

But you'll see us!

We shall nod at all your lectures
Then repurpose architecture
Creating art that lives and moves
Grinding every stopper smooth
We shall not be denied
We shall not run and hide
From Manchester to Southbank
We worship and give thanks
For we don't need or want approval
There shall be no removal
From these streets, steps or stairs.

You shall hear us.

It's not Hawk or Bam or Gonz
It's not heavenly half pipe songs
It's the sound of distant wheels
It's the nearing of our thrills
It's no Jackass style show
It's one more fucking go!
Its bloodied shins and sweat
It's not a moment to regret
It's bombing towards old age
It's a refusal to be caged

You'll never know us!

That thump and slump and resulting lump

Those limbs that point to impossible angles

That slip, that trip and that bruised hip

That leaves you broken, moaning and mangled

Those shins akin to broken things

Those knees that pop each time you stand

The bruise from a cruise that wasn't so smooth

The inconvenience of a broken hand

The price ain't nice for living this life

But that sound we hear as we roll away!

So, the crashes, the smashes and the griptape rashes

Are the cost of playing that we're happy to pay.

Illustration: Arron Campbell

gripped

You stand there, hang there, eyeing me from the wall
I spot you through the crowd of perfection
Yet you alone stand out.

Your silent serenity, promise of fidelity, whispers of what
could be.

Perhaps you'll be the one, the perfect choice, my escape.

I pick you or you pick me.
Whatever.
It happens.

I lay you down. I grip you (badly!)

I mount the hard parts on your firm underbelly.
I set you in motion with loving care.

You are the one. I plucked you and you thank me for choosing
you from all the others.

I take you to my special place.
Your hips ride the hips of Boadicea like nothing else in my mind.
Absolute perfection is promised.

I mount you.

You hold me.

At first.

Then you buck.

You're just like the rest!

I drag you home, I place you on the rack.

Another calls me from the crowd...

Illustration: Jason "Hillbilly" Chevera

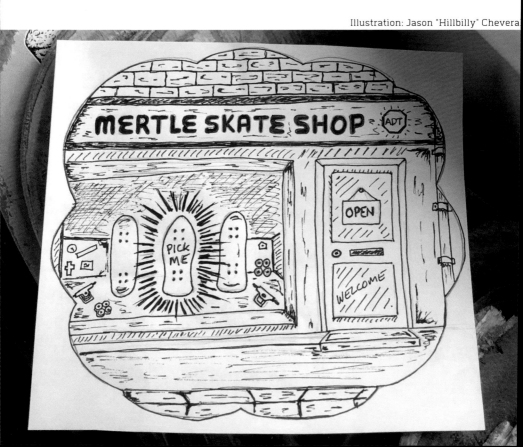

summer's promise

That smell is back again
Of warm wooden friends
The sun has them awake
Built and ready to skate
First sun has dried the bowls
Two minutes to banish the cold
A man, a toy and time
Summer promise, so sublime
Bowls that stay so dry
No more soggy ply
We emerge from underground
Blinking eyes look around
Adjust to summer's breeze
To ride wherever we please!
For the rain is in retreat
Our poly smells so sweet
Sweaty bum marks on our grip
Meets arranged super quick
Perhaps a beer at a park
A fire once it's dark
Stories swapped and told
New faces mixed with old
New tricks that leave us stoked
Encouraged by our FoUKS
The screen at which you stare
Has friends just waiting there
To meet, to come and play
Friendships made to stay!

That clackety-clack
Used to take me back
But now it brings me here
That skate shop smell
Back to how I felt
For many a happy year

And now I've returned
A few tricks relearned
I've rediscovered play
I've made friends anew
We're the living proof
That the past is ours today!

From far and wide
We come to ride
In groups or all alone
With a passion shared
For what once was there
For a history that we own!

So, join me friends
'til the bitter end
Raise your decks and shout
We shan't just observe
Because we deserve
To roll until our knees give out!

scape from

oredom

Once upon a time there was a man with no story
He'd never had the guts to win any glory
He never left the path that led him home safe
Never had the balls to take a leap of faith
A steady income job working for a boss
Never took a chance, so never had a loss
Never broke a bone or scabbed his knees as a man
Stuck to what he knew and stuck to the grand plan

Then he heard a clatter
His mind began to chatter
Faster than a mad hatter

And a skater whizzed by
He wondered then just why
He'd let his dreams all die?

Life got in the way
He'd forgotten how to play
Chose a path that was safe

And as that skater disappeared

His foggy mind began to clear

Escaped from boredom with some fear

A deck was bought to ride

And with nowhere left to hide

He took his toy outside

Two years on down the line

If you search you can find

A man living outside his mind

Illustration: Jason 'Hillbilly' Cheverall

New friends

Yeah, he's rocking Vans and sometimes it's Airwalks
An Independent tee and skater lingo talk.
He likes to say 'dude' or 'gnarly' or 'rad'
Doesn't own a skateboard and that makes him quite sad.
He looks at old pictures of days long since gone
The smell of piss at Southbank and overcrowded Rom
That urge to skate again just can't be held at bay
An overwhelming need to just go out and play

But he's old.
He's got a mortgage.
He's overweight.
People will laugh.

So, he has a look on Facebook out of curiosity
Images assault him, blinded by what he sees
A thousand other men still rolling on their planks
Who rediscovered fun, beyond golf and half-arsed wanks!
So now he's gonna meet some, at his old stomping ground
He's nervous like a new kid but they turn out to be sound.

He's made new friends.
Friends of friends.
New friends in his forties!

The Airwalk T shirt's gone now, replaced with Moonshine
He doesn't skate T Bones much, rides a pop most of the time
Wednesdays are his skate night but that's not set in stone
Whenever the chance comes, he grabs his ride and leaves his home.
That fat man buying t shirts online or at TK Maxx
Would never have believed what skating gave him back!

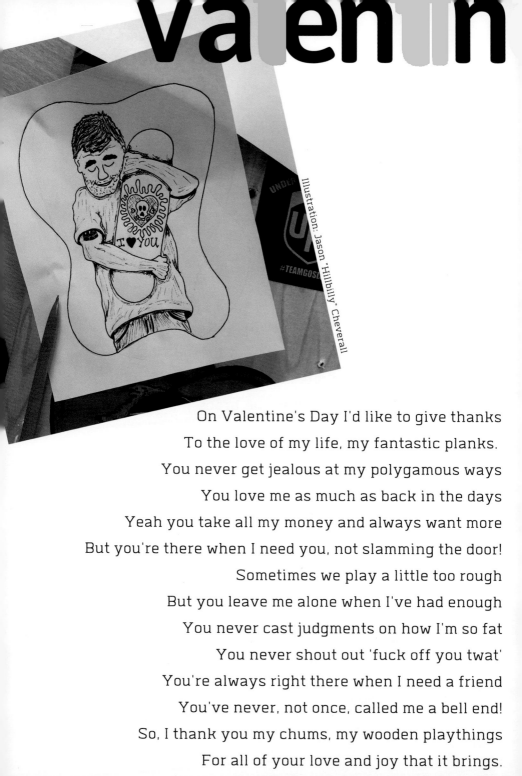

Illustration: Jason 'Hillbilly' Cheverall

On Valentine's Day I'd like to give thanks
To the love of my life, my fantastic planks.
You never get jealous at my polygamous ways
You love me as much as back in the days
Yeah you take all my money and always want more
But you're there when I need you, not slamming the door!
Sometimes we play a little too rough
But you leave me alone when I've had enough
You never cast judgments on how I'm so fat
You never shout out 'fuck off you twat'
You're always right there when I need a friend
You've never, not once, called me a bell end!
So, I thank you my chums, my wooden playthings
For all of your love and joy that it brings.

I broke my arm
I popped my knee
I rolled my ankle
I watched me bleed

I blacked my eye
I twisted fingers
On winter mornings
My pains all linger

But for all my pains
I truly feel
Nothing compares
To the bruised heel!

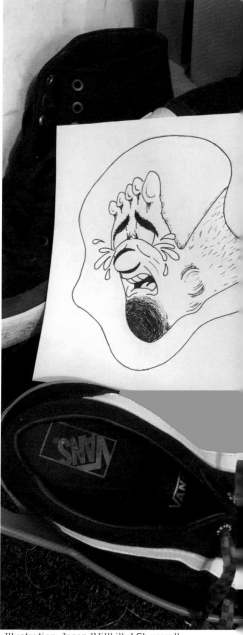

Illustration: Jason "Hillbilly" Cheverall

Bruised he

Fat smile

We adapt and move and throw arms aloft
(Well, they do, I just fall off!)

Shuffle feet like lightning and alter our stance
(Not me, I slam at every chance!)

Of the board they become an absolute master
(Not me obviously, I'm a total disaster)

We kick, flip and spin and still roll away
(But I'm on my knees yet again like every day!)

We have skills, we have fun, we have style for miles
(Not me but I do have a big fat smile)

My eye is blackened from love
Smashed to the ground from above
But it's not her fault!
My hips burn from the bruises
As I make my excuses
My nerves are fraught!

I tried to walk away but returned
From punishment nothing is learned
So, I skulk back.
This dark mistress of mine
Whispers I'll be fine
Before the attack.

And like a fool I believe her lies
As she blackens each of my eyes
But I'm to blame
For all the pain she inflicts
With her vicious tricks
Addicted to this game.

So, I come back for even more
I'll be better than before
Her siren song calling
She lulls me with her charm
She causes so much harm
My love for skateboarding

Dark mistress

Next Time

I hit the ground hard
Fell my bone shard
From an old injury
To one of my fucked knees.

Next time.

This time I do the splits
I'm sure something's ripped
But I hobble to my feet
No glory in defeat.

This time.

Hope I don't break it
Don't hurt when you make it
But I wouldn't know
So, one more go.

This time. Please!

I'm sure I've got it
But I eat more shit
Scrape myself up
Ignoring all my blood.

This fucking time!

By the end of the day
I roll it away
Broken but I'm fine
Until next time.

eabegger

It isn't lessons or rules or a need to be cool

It isn't drugs and bongs and hip-hop songs

It isn't a punk ass attitude when spitting and being crude

It's not the competition or stupid bitching

It's not the cleanest lines or best designs

It ain't about winning or losing or flipping or cruising

It's not beer with your friends and it don't depend

On who's got what or who's top dog

It ain't anything above.

It's about pure love.

It's not making that trick

It's about just doing it.

No bigger goal than living to roll.

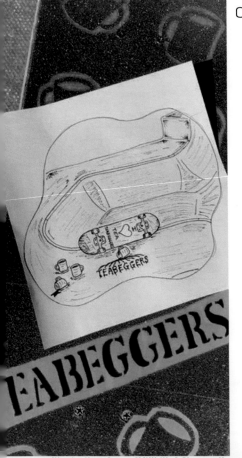

Illustration: Jason "Hillbilly" Cheverall

Escape in to skating

Let the world fadeaway

Living not just waiting

Work so I can play

Escaping from the hoards

With just this toy at my feet

Ignore the news abroad

Calm my heartbeat

This is my salvation

This is my balm

Pure recreation

A form of self-harm?

self-harm

Rubbing bone

Not much left but rubbing bones
Shattered bodies and gravelly moans

Riding planks with wind in our hair
Well, what's left, not much up there

Fingers bent and thumbs worn rough
Gripping our dreams in a vice so tough

We broken warriors that have returned
Or never left those lessons learned

And I know now the cost of pounds
Cos, I don't bounce when I hit the ground

We lay on the flat with nowhere to hide
Except behind smiles, a mile wide

We all limp back to our homesteads
Battered and broken but not quite dead

And tomorrow we know that as we're waking
We shall find a surprise piece of us aching

And we shall smile at those aches and pains
And look forward to when once again

We ride our planks up a wall, ramp or rail
And enjoy the makes and falls and fails.

Doesn't matter where you've been or even where you're going
Your life's on display in the scars you are showing
Everything is aching but the sun is on your back
So, live for this moment and cut yourself some slack
Ride through those emotions and don't over think
Skating is a potion and we've all had a drink.
Escape from the life that has you dutybound
Remember when it was fun to lay upon the ground?

With old scabs bleeding and new cuts screaming
Shins on fire from decks that are speeding!

You'd dust yourself down, ignore physical harm
Carry on skating, picking gravel out your palm.

This is what we do and its grip is like a vice
It smashed us to bits, it annoys the poor wife!
But you can't stop now! You're a skater for life!

Scars

Take flight my plank of joy
Reduce me back to that scabby-kneed boy
Spin beneath me on winds unseen
With invisible strings make lines so clean

I'm sorry I left you wherever you may be
But know I still love you! Do you love me?
My wooden friends I used to caress
Abandoned in search of adultness
I believed this hunt was for wooden toys
I knew I was wrong when I heard that noise

So, I apologise now for ever eloping
For we are a heaven made match
when we grind the coping
Sparks do fly and sounds abound
As together we try to leave the ground

I'll fall on my face and I might break bones
I'll roll my ankles and slam on stones

I'll tear my jeans and land on my arse
And nowadays I don't heal fast!

But for as long as I can, while body allows
I'll say I'm a skater and I'll say it proud!

For one brief moment just cast it all aside
The anger and the spite, the pointless brainwashed pride.
Come with me my brothers, on platforms we shall stand
And when you slide away, you're pulled back by loving hands.

There are roofs we need to fix and bills to be paid
We're chained to our jobs with children to be raised.

But for just a day or two we can escape this rat race
We fling away our problems, we have our own space.

Like an excited child when your best mate called
And said to you my friend 'let's go and skateboard!'

Playing ou

Paradise Cove where nobody goes
Away from home and all alone
I've claimed this slice
This paradise
Where escaping the chaos feels so nice.

This deserted place is Paradise Cove
This slice of nirvana I call home
I'll build my nest where I feel safe
Paradise Cove such a blissed-out place.

Across the bluest seas I'll be back next year
Paradise Cove absorbs all my fears
I think you'd like it, give it a try
Come with me and you'll see why.

Paradise Cove where nobody goes
Away from home and all alone
I've claimed this slice
This paradise
Where escaping the chaos feels so nice.

I'll open a bar right here, on the beach
Where civilisation is out of reach
And share this cove with the one I love
We'll lay together with just blue above.

Just above the bar I'll build a room
In keeping with surroundings, nothing rude.
I'll rent it out for a nominal fee
Just a couple of tourists, you and me.

Paradise Cove where nobody goes
Away from home and all alone
I've claimed this slice
This paradise
Where escaping the chaos feels so nice.

Next year they'll come back these wacked out slackers
And they'll probably bring a few backpackers
So, my bar gets bigger and before you know
I've added more rooms and a casino...

Paradise Cove has made me rich
But all these tourists make me itch
I wanna escape this rat race beach
As my personal heaven spins out of reach.

Paradise Cove where nobody goes
Away from home and all alone
I've claimed this slice
This paradise
Where escaping the chaos feels so nice.

Paradise Cove where everyone goes
Invading my home, I'm never alone
They've claimed this slice
This ex paradise
I want to escape but the money's nice.

Paradise Cov

Like a laid back beauty with beckoning eyes

This temptress calls me and whispers 'ride'

Seductive curves naked as can be

I strain at the leash that's slowly choking me

Every inch exposed, every hip, every curve

The sun upon her back, she's more than I deserve.

Oh I know she's had others but now it's just us

Yet I'm forbidden this fruit, strangled by my lust

It would be oh so easy to cheat upon the rules

Stinky Virus Prickhips

To simply dive into her eyes like welcoming pools

To lose myself of worries for just a little time

For never the chance shall come again for her to be just mine

I know how she'd feel, it would be heavenly

But a shitting dog destroys my reverie!

Poo bag in hand instead of a board

I bid farewell to my sexy broad

But I shall return when isolation ends

And share my love with selected friends.

Illustration: Arron Campbell